LIVING THINGS

ROBERT SNEDDEN

Birds

A⁺

Smart Apple Media

Published by Smart Apple Media
2140 Howard Drive West
North Mankato, MN 56003

Designed by Guy Callaby
Edited by Pip Morgan
Illustrations by Guy Callaby
Picture research by Su Alexander

Picture acknowledgements
Title page Doug Wechsler/Nature Picture Library; 3 Hanne & Jens Eriksen/Nature Picture
Library; 4 Tony Heald/Nature Picture Library; 5l Pete Oxford/Nature Picture Library, r Eric
Baccega/Nature Picture Library; 7t Galen Rowell/Corbis, b Colin Seddon/Nature Picture
Library; 8 Bernard Castelein/Nature Picture Library; 9 Darrell Gulin/Corbis; 10 Jeff Vanuga/
Corbis; 11 Doug Allan/Nature Picture Library; 12 Tony Heald/Nature Picture Library;
14 Dave Watts/Nature Picture Library; 15 Adam White/Nature Picture Library; 17t Pete
Oxford/Nature Picture Library, b Jeff Foott/Nature Picture Library; 18 David Kjaer/Nature
Picture Library; 19t Rolf Nussbaumer/Nature Picture Library, b Pete Oxford/Nature Picture
Library; 20 Doug Wechsler/Nature Picture Library; 21t Bengt Lundberg/Nature Picture
Library b Eric Hosking/Corbis; 22 Horst Ossinger/DPA/Corbis; 23t Phil Savoie/Nature
Picture Library, b Barry Mansell/Nature Picture Library; 24 Kim Taylor/Nature Picture
Library; 25 Brian Lightfoot/Nature Picture Library; 26 Colin Seddon/Nature Picture Library;
27t Rolf Nussbaumer/Nature Picture Library, b Hanne & Jens Eriksen/Nature Picture
Library; 28 Tom Mangelsen/Nature Picture Library; 29 Frank Lukasseck/ZEFA/Corbis:

Front cover W.Perry Conway/Corbis

Printed in China

Library of Congress Cataloging-in-Publication Data

Snedden, Robert.
Birds / by Robert Snedden.
p. cm. — (Living things)
Includes index.
ISBN-13: 978-1-59920-076-7
1. Birds—Juvenile literature. I. Title.

QL676.2.S614 2007
598—dc22   2006031885

First Edition

9 8 7 6 5 4 3 2 1

Contents

What is a bird?

You probably have a pretty good idea what a bird is already. We share the world with many wild animals, but birds are usually the ones we see and hear the most. Even in the middle of cities there are birds, whether they are flocks of pigeons or an occasional hawk. We eat many birds as food, and we keep some as pets.

A riot of birds

Birds come in a wide variety of shapes, sizes, and colors. From elegant pink flamingoes and waddling penguins to soaring eagles and squawking parrots, birds make the world a noisier and more colorful place. They are all different, yet they are all birds.

BELOW
Lammergeiers live in the mountains of southern Europe and in Africa. They drop bones from a great height to crack them open, so they can eat the marrow inside.

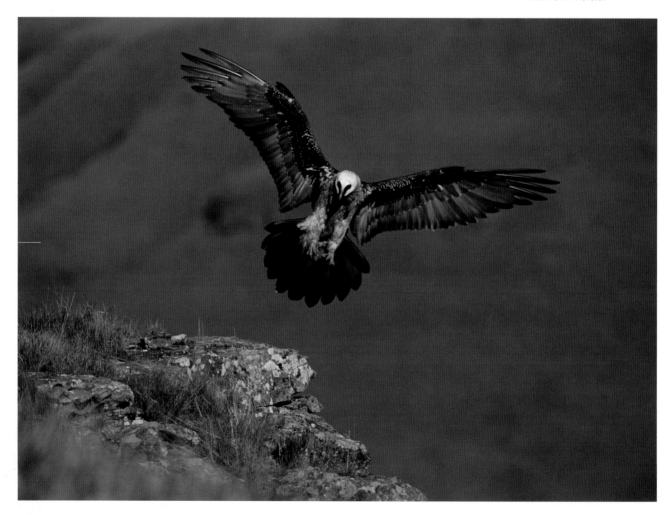

The smallest bird in the world is the bee hummingbird, which is just over two inches (6 cm) long and weighs less than 0.07 ounces (2 g). The heaviest flying bird is the great bustard, which can weigh over 44 pounds (20 kg).

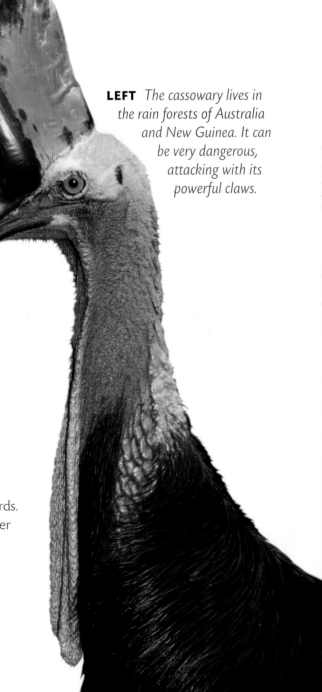

LEFT *The cassowary lives in the rain forests of Australia and New Guinea. It can be very dangerous, attacking with its powerful claws.*

ABOVE *This male frigate from the Galapagos Islands in the Pacific Ocean attracts the attention of a female by puffing up his bright red throat pouch.*

Eggs and wings

What makes a bird different from other animals? We might say that a bird is an animal that flies and lays eggs. Bats fly, but they don't lay eggs, so they aren't birds. Penguins don't fly, but they do lay eggs and they are birds. Frogs and fish lay eggs, but they definitely aren't birds. Alligators make nests for their eggs, but they aren't birds, either.

What makes a bird a bird and not something else? This book will help you find out about the remarkable living creatures we call birds. You'll discover some of the things they have in common with other animals—and just what it is that makes them special.

Birds and feathers

Birds are the only animals that have feathers. So if an animal has feathers, then it is a bird.

All birds, from parrots to penguins, have feathers. A bird's feathers are very important. They keep it warm and dry and help cushion its body from injury. Feathers may be camouflaged to hide the bird from predators, or brightly colored to attract a mate. Without feathers, a bird cannot fly.

barb

barbule

hook

shaft

shaft

outer

FLIGHT FEATHER

VANE STRUCTURE
Vanes are made up of barbs that branch off the shaft of the feather. Barbules branch off the barbs and are held in place by rows of hooks.

inner vane

quill

Plumage
All of a bird's feathers combined are called the plumage. There are two main types of feathers: contour feathers and down feathers. Down feathers lie next to the bird's skin. They are soft and fluffy, and they hold air to keep the bird warm. Young birds only have down feathers when they are born.

As a bird grows older, it begins to grow contour feathers. Contour feathers look flat and smooth. They are arranged in regular rows on the body and overlap each other so there are no gaps between them. The contour feathers give the bird its shape and also its color. Specially shaped contour feathers, called flight feathers, make up the bird's wings and tail; these feathers enable it to fly.

Feather structure

Feathers are made from the same material as the scales of reptiles and your nails and hair. This is a strong, lightweight, and flexible substance called keratin. A hollow central shaft runs down the middle of each feather and attaches it to the bird's body. The softer vanes of the feather grow out in two rows on either side of the shaft.

Contour feathers have many tiny hooks that fasten the vanes together, keeping the feather flat and smooth. Down feathers don't have these hooks so they stay fluffy.

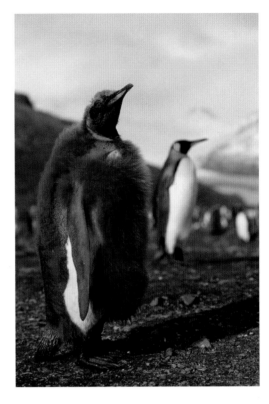

RIGHT *This young king penguin chick begins to lose its downy juvenile feathers as it gains its adult plumage.*

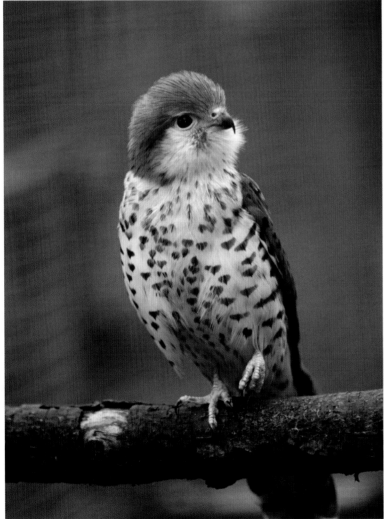

LEFT *The speckled breast of this Mauritius kestrel clearly shows how the contour feathers neatly overlap each other.*

WOW!

The longest feathers ever seen were on a chicken in Japan. Its tail feathers measured 34.7 feet (10.59 m) long! The bird with the most feathers is the whistling swan, which has around 25,000 feathers.

Feather care

A bird couldn't survive long without its feathers. So it takes great care of them and keeps them in good condition.

Preening

Feathers, particularly the contour feathers of the wings, need to be kept smooth and flat and in the right place. The bird does this by running its beak along the feathers and nibbling at the edges. This is called preening. It helps rid the feathers of any dirt and also makes sure that the tiny hooks linking the feather vanes are all connected.

Many birds can also waterproof their feathers. They have a preen gland near their tail. This produces an oily substance that the bird spreads over its feathers while it is preening. The oil helps keep the feathers flexible.

BELOW *The kingfisher waterproofs its feathers to prevent them from becoming soaked with water when it dives to catch a fish.*

Powder down

Birds that don't have preen glands grow special feathers called powder down on their breasts. These feathers grow all the time. Their tips break down into a fine waterproof powder that the bird spreads over its feathers in the same way that other birds use oil from their preen gland. Water birds, such as egrets and herons, have large amounts of powder down. Most birds have some, even those with preen glands.

Molting

No amount of care can keep feathers from wearing out or being damaged. Birds regularly lose old feathers and replace them with new ones. This is called molting. The old feathers are pushed out by the new ones growing beneath them. A small bird can grow new feathers in a month or two, but a large bird, such as an eagle, may take a few years to completely change its plumage.

ABOVE *The great egret collects powder down from its breast. It will use this powder to waterproof its feathers.*

WOW!

Water birds, such as ducks and swans, lose their flight feathers all at once. They can't fly for several weeks until the new feathers grow.

Wings—but not for flying

Another thing all birds have in common is that they have wings. Birds' wings come in a variety of shapes and sizes. Most birds use their wings for one very obvious purpose—to fly. However, some birds do not fly, but they still use their wings.

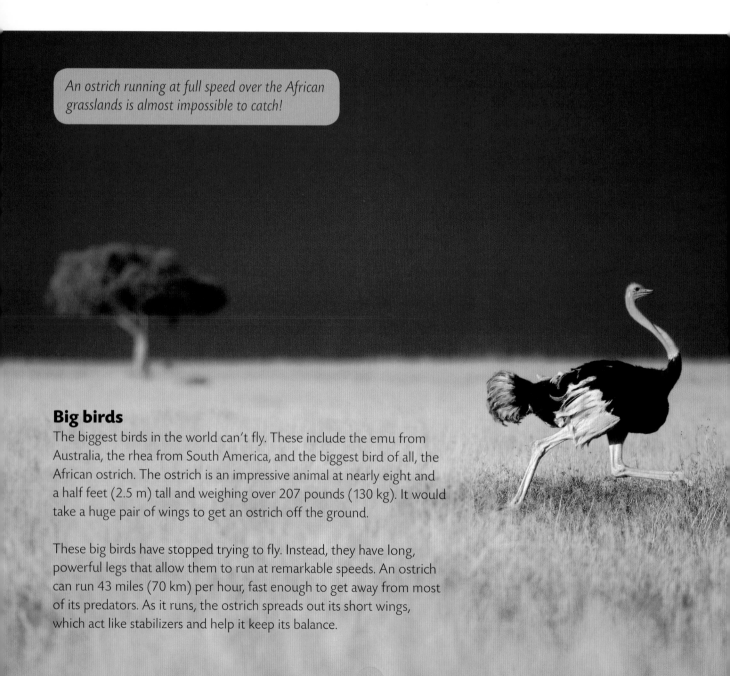

An ostrich running at full speed over the African grasslands is almost impossible to catch!

Big birds

The biggest birds in the world can't fly. These include the emu from Australia, the rhea from South America, and the biggest bird of all, the African ostrich. The ostrich is an impressive animal at nearly eight and a half feet (2.5 m) tall and weighing over 207 pounds (130 kg). It would take a huge pair of wings to get an ostrich off the ground.

These big birds have stopped trying to fly. Instead, they have long, powerful legs that allow them to run at remarkable speeds. An ostrich can run 43 miles (70 km) per hour, fast enough to get away from most of its predators. As it runs, the ostrich spreads out its short wings, which act like stabilizers and help it keep its balance.

Flying underwater

Like ostriches and emus, penguins are birds that do not fly. But unlike ostriches and emus, penguins are not very good at running. A torpedo-shaped penguin may look amusing as it waddles over the snow, but it is just the right shape for moving smoothly through water. Penguins are great swimmers. A penguin's wings are called flippers and are shorter and harder than the wings of flying birds. Penguin wings are shaped like paddles, and they are very useful for speeding through the water.

ABOVE *Emperor penguins are the champion divers of the bird world. They can reach depths of 1,640 feet (500 m) in search of food. The greatest depth ever reached by a human without breathing equipment is 564 feet (172 m).*

Kiwis and kakapos

New Zealand is home to two of the world's most unusual birds. The chicken-sized kiwi is a shy and secretive forest dweller. It has very small wings and no tail at all. During the day, kiwis hide in burrows or under logs, emerging at night to eat berries and bugs on the forest floor. They might not be able to fly, but they can outrun most humans!

The kakapo is a very special bird. It is the world's heaviest parrot, weighing up to 8.8 pounds (4.4 kg). It is the only parrot in the world that is active at night and the only parrot that can't fly. It is also the world's rarest parrot—there are fewer than one hundred left. Kakapos are good climbers and use their wings to balance on tree branches.

Built for flight

Most birds are built to fly and to spend at least some of their lives in the air. All birds have a pair of wings instead of front legs or arms, and a flying bird has powerful breast muscles, light bones, big lungs, and a large heart.

Liftoff!

Flying through the air requires a lot of strength. When a bird takes off it has to lift itself into the air by sheer muscle power. Birds have powerful breast muscles to give themselves that first strong beat of the wings which lifts them off the ground. The breast muscles of birds such as pigeons can make up one-third of the bird's total weight.

Pumping power

Just like your heart, a bird's heart pumps oxygen-rich blood around the body to where it is needed. A bird's heart is big and strong and has a structure similar to a mammal's heart. In relation to its body weight, a bird's heart is bigger than a mammal's.

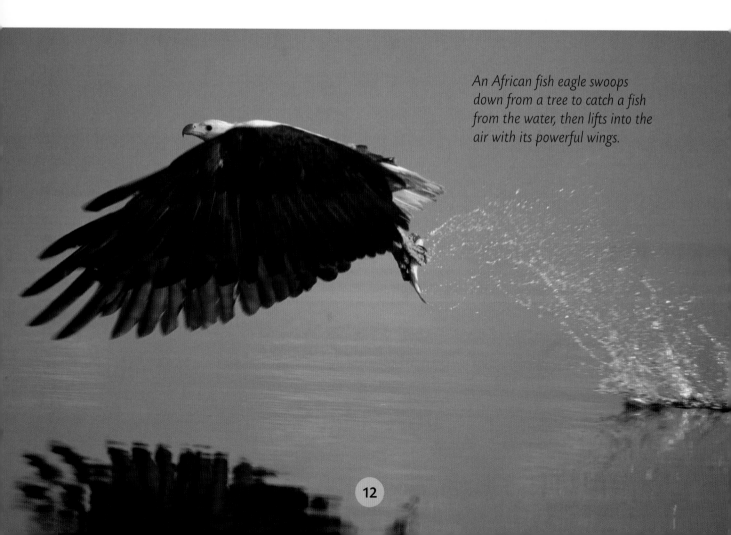

An African fish eagle swoops down from a tree to catch a fish from the water, then lifts into the air with its powerful wings.

BIRD SKELETON

A bird's skeleton has several adaptations for flight, including a light skull without teeth or heavy jawbones, a wishbone to support the wings, and a large sternum to anchor the big flight muscles.

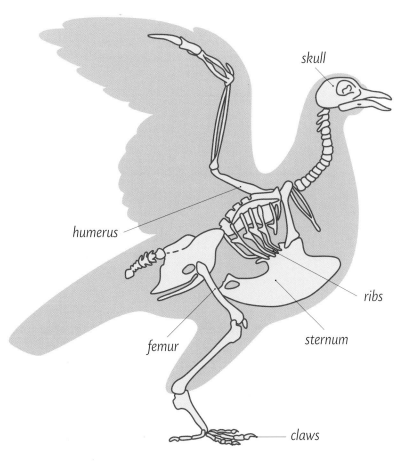

skull

humerus

femur

claws

sternum

ribs

Hollow bones

Weight is an important factor in flying. The heavier the bird, the more power it needs to fly. Birds are adapted to weigh as little as possible. They have very light, hollow bones and do not have many of the bones that other animals have. The skeletons of some birds actually weigh less than their feathers do!

What's that splat?

Birds also weigh less because they do not have bladders to store urine. Rather than producing liquid urine to get rid of wastes, birds produce a white, paste-like substance. That's what a bird dropping is!

Air supply

Flying takes a lot of energy—much more than walking or running. This means that a bird needs a good supply of oxygen to help it release energy from food. A bird's lungs are much more complicated and efficient than those of mammals, such as humans. The lungs also take up much more space in a bird's body. Your lungs compose about one-twentieth of your body, but a bird's make up about one-fifth.

BIRD RESPIRATORY SYSTEM

Birds have two lungs and nine air sacs—five sacs at the front and four at the rear. Some of the front sacs are inside hollow bones.

The bird breathes in through the trachea to fill the rear air sacs with fresh, oxygen-rich air. This air is then squeezed from the rear air sacs into the lungs. Oxygen passes from the lungs into the bloodstream, leaving behind stale air. The stale air then moves from the lungs into the front air sacs, and the bird breathes it out of the front air sacs through the trachea.

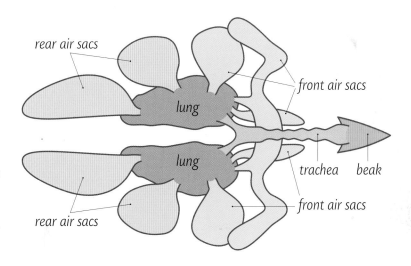

rear air sacs

front air sacs

lung

lung

trachea   beak

front air sacs

rear air sacs

13

Wings for flying

Once a bird has propelled itself up into the air it has to stay there. What keeps a bird from fluttering back down to the ground again?

Lift and drag

Take a sheet of paper and hold it loosely by the edge so that it flops down in front of you. Now blow hard across the top of the paper (not underneath it). Watch how the air flowing across the paper makes it rise. The air flowing over the paper results in an upward force called lift.

Birds and airplanes both stay up in the air by creating lift. A bird creates lift by flapping its wings to make the air flow over them. The engines of an airplane create lift by pushing it forward and forcing the air to flow over its wings.

Air doesn't just keep the bird up, however. Air resistance also slows the bird down as it flies forward. This is called drag. A bird's wings are shaped to cut as smoothly as possible through the air. The bird also holds its wings at an angle to make sure that it gets as much lift as possible.

Hovering hummingbirds

Hummingbirds can hover in one spot. A hovering hummingbird has no air flowing over its wings to give lift. Instead, it keeps itself up by beating its wings very rapidly forward and backward. Its wings twist around so they are always pushing the bird upward. By tilting its wings, a hummingbird can fly in any direction. It can even fly upside down for a second or two!

The broad-billed hummingbird is a frequent summer visitor to gardens in the southwestern U.S.

BIRD WING

A bird's wing is made of primary and secondary feathers with smaller feathers called coverts covering the place where the primaries attach to the wing.

- Primaries
- Secondaries
- Primary coverts
- Secondary coverts

digits

humerus

Primaries and secondaries

The feathers that make up a bird's wing are not all the same. Primary feathers propel the bird through the air. Usually, birds have ten of these primaries on each wing. They are attached to bones that, in humans, would be the hand. A bird is unable to fly if its primaries are lost or damaged.

Secondary wing feathers are attached to bones similar to the forearm in humans. Secondaries shape the wing into an ideal surface for flying and form the main surface that air flows over, giving lift.

WOW!

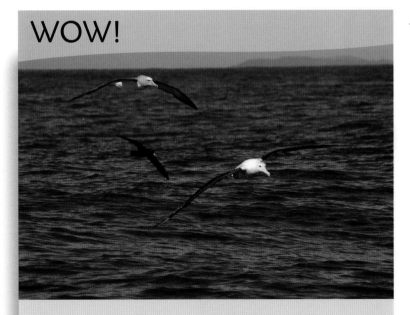

The wandering albatross has the longest wings in the world. Some have wingspans of over 11 feet (3.5 m). The highest flying bird is the griffon vulture. In 1973, one collided with an airplane more than 6.8 miles (11,000 m) above the Ivory Coast in Africa.

Bird digestion

Birds use a lot of energy, which means they need a lot of food. When they're awake, most birds spend much of their time looking for something to eat. Many birds consume one-fifth of their body weight in food every day to get the energy they need. Imagine how you'd feel if you had to eat that much.

Crop storage

When you swallow your food it goes down a tube and into your stomach. In birds, this tube has an enlarged section called the crop where food can be stored for later if the stomach is full. A bird can also use its crop to carry food to its chicks. Another advantage is that the crop allows a bird to eat swiftly and then fly to a safe place to digest its meal.

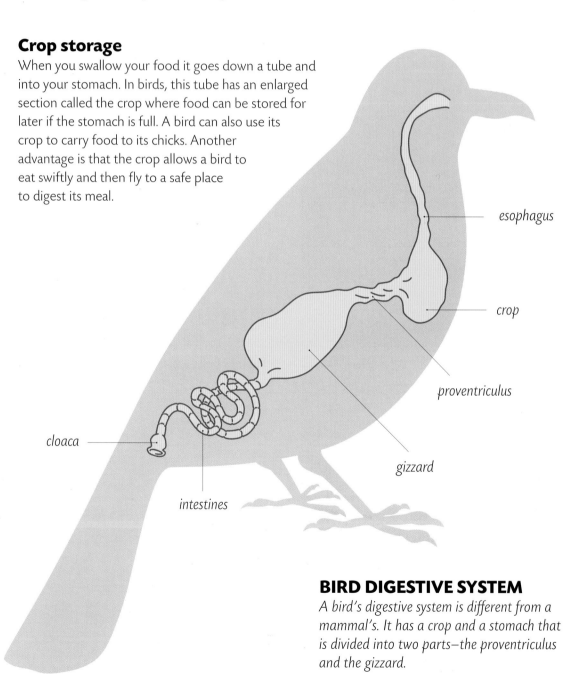

esophagus

crop

proventriculus

gizzard

cloaca

intestines

BIRD DIGESTIVE SYSTEM

A bird's digestive system is different from a mammal's. It has a crop and a stomach that is divided into two parts—the proventriculus and the gizzard.

Grinding gizzards

Birds have no teeth and cannot chew their food. They must either swallow it whole or use their beak to crack or tear it into pieces. A two-part stomach helps a bird's digestive process.

The first part of the stomach begins to break down the food using digestive juices. The second part, or gizzard, has very powerful muscles that grind up the bird's food. To get an idea of how powerful the gizzard is, try squeezing a walnut shell between your fingers. A turkey's gizzard is strong enough to crush the walnut! Sometimes, birds swallow small stones that stay in the gizzard, helping the grinding process.

Birds of prey use their gizzards to store indigestible parts of their food, such as bones and fur. This becomes a pellet that the bird eventually spits out.

End of the line

Once the food has been pulverized and dissolved by the stomach, it passes into the intestines. From here, all the nutrients from the food are absorbed into the bloodstream and transported to the rest of the bird's body. Your intestines work in much the same way. The bird's digestive system ends at the cloaca. Here, anything left over that couldn't be digested is stored before being expelled.

Bills and beaks

A bird doesn't have arms and hands to help it lift or carry something. If it wants to pick up anything, it has to use its feet or its bill. Is it a bill or is it a beak? There's no difference really—they're just two words for the same thing.

Almost all the work of feeding is done by the bill. Looking at a bird's bill tells you a lot about the sort of food it eats. For instance, hummingbirds have long beaks to reach the nectar in flowers, like drinking through a straw. Woodpeckers have bills like sharp chisels that they use to chip away at tree trunks to find insects hiding there. Ducks and flamingos have bills that strain tiny animals and plant material out of water.

BELOW *The strong, hooked bill of the common buzzard marks it as a predator that is able to tear strips from its prey.*

Bills and jaws

A bird's bill is not the same thing as an animal's jaw. The bill is actually a horny covering over the bird's jaw. Birds have very lightweight jaws compared to those of reptiles and mammals, which helps make flying easier for them.

Swiss Army bills

A bird's bill has to do many things—a bit like a Swiss Army knife! In addition to eating food, the bill might catch food, probe or dig for it, scoop it from water, or carry it to the nest. Birds use their bills to care for their feathers, to fetch materials for their nests, and to defend themselves. When they hatch, birds use their bills to peck through the eggshell, into the world.

BELOW *The flamingo collects tiny plants and animals from the water by scooping water into its bill and filtering it back out through slits in its beak and bristles on its tongue.*

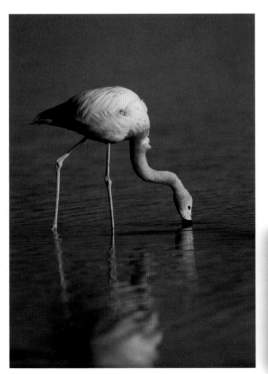

Hunting and fishing

Hunting birds, such as hawks and eagles, have strong beaks that are thick and curved with sharp hooks that they use to tear at their prey. Herons and egrets have long, spear-like beaks that they use to catch fish. Pelicans dive under water and scoop fish into the bottom of their big beaks, like catching them in a net.

Seed eaters

Seed-eating birds, such as sparrows and finches, have hard, cone-shaped beaks that can vary a great deal. Some birds eat tiny seeds and have small bills to match. Others have heavy bills combined with powerful jaw muscles that can crack big seeds, such as cherry stones.

ABOVE *A curlew uses its long bill to probe beneath the surface of mudflats for small animals to eat.*

WOW!

The Australian pelican has the longest bill in the world. It is nearly two feet (0.5 m) in length. The sword-billed hummingbird, with its 3.9-inch (10 cm) long bill, is the only bird with a bill that's longer than its body.

Songs and calls

One of the first things that might spring to mind when you think about birds is their singing. Not all birds sing, and people find some birds' songs more pleasant than others. However, when a bird sings, it is singing for other reasons beside our pleasure.

I'm here!

Birds call and sing to communicate with other birds. Among songbirds, the male sings most often. One of the things he is saying is, "This is my place. You stay away!" He is telling other birds like him that this is his territory. In the spring, males also hope to attract a mate with their singing.

BELOW *A male western meadowlark sings out–perhaps to attract a mate, warn off rivals, or both! The bird spends each summer in North America and flies south in the winter.*

The voice box

Near the top of your throat is the larynx, or voice box. When you speak or sing, the voice box vibrates to produce different sounds. The voice box of a bird is called a syrinx. It is shaped like an upside down "Y" and located at the bottom of a bird's throat throat. Here the syrinx splits to join the lungs so there are two parts that vibrate to make sound. This means that the bird has two different ways to make sound, rather than just the one way that we have. The two sources of sound blend together, producing a complex variety of sounds.

Not all birds have a syrinx, and some have a syrinx that is undeveloped. For example, some vultures don't have one and can only make various hissing and grunting noises.

The language of birds

Most birds have a number of calls they use to send messages to one another. There are many reasons why birds call. A hungry chick in the nest will call to its parents to be fed. In a large seabird colony, a returning parent can find its own chick by recognizing its call. Chicks also have distress calls that they make to alert their parents of danger.

Birds that fly in flocks communicate with each other by calling. For example, a flocking call can bring a scattered group of birds back together again.

ABOVE *Chicks, such as these great tits, call to get attention when a parent returns with food.*

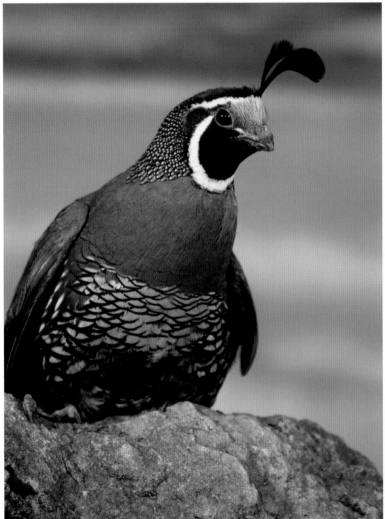

LEFT *When a flock of California quails is feeding, one will stand guard ready to give a loud call to alert the other birds to any danger.*

WOW!

The song of a European wren is made of more than 700 different notes a minute and can be heard 1,650 feet (500 m) away.

Look at me!

Some birds are rather drab and dull. Others appear very bright and colorful. Sometimes we see these differences in the same kind of bird. Male birds draw attention to themselves with their showy feathers, while the females are much more plain. What is the reason for this?

Breeding plumage

Most of the time the male is brightly colored to try to attract the attention of a mate. The message here is, "Look at me! See how fit and healthy I am." The male birds with the brightest, most spectacular plumage are the ones that are most attractive to the females.

At the same time, the male is sending a message to rival males. He is showing them how good he is at defending his territory, and his eye-catching visual display is often accompanied by loud singing.

BELOW *The contrast is extraordinary between the bright blue male peacock with his immense tail and the drab brown female peahen.*

A male bird trying to attract a female risks attracting the attention of a predator, too. However, some males don't seem to care. One example is the group known as birds of paradise, which are members of the crow family. The males are some of the most colorful birds on earth. While showing off their bright plumage, they cry loudly and perform vigorous dances on the forest floor. They are definitely attention grabbers!

Camouflage nesting

Female birds usually take care of the eggs in the nest. It wouldn't be a good idea for the female to draw the attention of hunting animals to herself and her eggs. A brightly

colored female would be much easier to see than a drab, brown bird. The female's feathers help camouflage her by blending in with the environment and making her difficult to see. When the chicks hatch, they are drab like their mother so they cannot be easily seen. A young bird's drab plumage doesn't only camouflage it. If the father bird visits the nest, the chick's plain coloring tells him that the young bird is harmless, and not a competing rival that has to be attacked and driven away.

ABOVE *This Wilson's plover and its eggs are both well camouflaged in its shoreline habitat in Key Largo, Florida.*

Laying eggs

All female birds lay eggs. Birds are not the only animals to lay eggs. Insects, fish, amphibians, and reptiles all lay eggs, too. But birds are especially careful with their eggs.

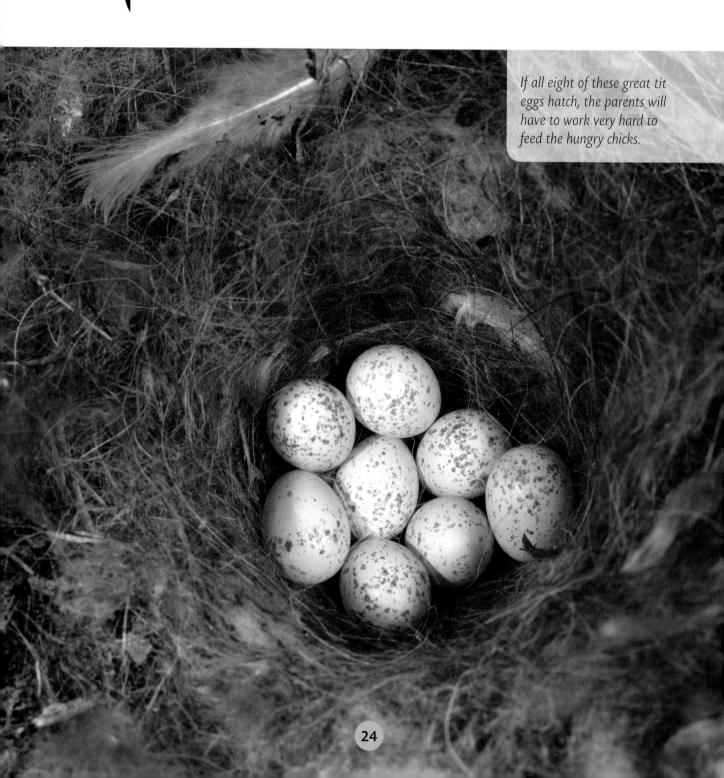

If all eight of these great tit eggs hatch, the parents will have to work very hard to feed the hungry chicks.

Life support

A bird's egg is like a life-support system for the chick. The egg provides both food and protection for the growing young bird that is inside. The eggshell contains calcium, a substance also found in bones. Female birds have a special kind of bone that they use to store the calcium they need for their eggs. It takes about 15 hours for a hen's egg to form inside her body.

Eggshells are waterproof but not airtight. Thousands of tiny holes in the shell let air pass back and forth, so the chick inside receives the oxygen it needs and waste gases can escape. Inside the egg, there is a yellow yolk surrounded by clear egg white, or albumen. The yolk is the chick's food supply. The albumen acts like a cushion to protect the chick. It is also a source of water.

Why lay eggs?

There is a good reason birds lay eggs rather than give birth to live young. Birds often lay several eggs over a period of a few days. If she had to carry her growing young inside her, a female bird would find it hard to get off the ground, making her vulnerable to predators. Another advantage of eggs is that the father can help care for them, although not all father birds do!

The number of eggs varies from one bird to another. A giant albatross, for example, lays one egg every other year. If conditions are good and food is plentiful, a European blackbird may lay a clutch, or group, of five eggs four times in one year.

ABOVE *The young chick has to peck its way out of the egg when it is ready to hatch. Here, a young lesser black-backed gull is about to make an appearance on May Island in Scotland.*

WOW!

The world's smallest bird eggs are the vervain hummingbird's eggs, weighing just over one-hundredth of an ounce (0.3 g). The ostrich lays the biggest eggs—about 3.3 pounds (1.5 kg) each. However, the champion egg layer is the kiwi. Her eggs are a quarter of her own weight—the equivalent of an ostrich laying an 88-pound (40 kg) egg!

*Ostrich egg
7 inches (18 cm) tall,
5.5 inches (14 cm) wide*

*Vervain hummingbird egg
0.5 inches (1.3 cm) tall,
0.3 inches (0.8 cm) wide*

Building nests

Most birds make nests to protect their eggs from bad weather and predators. The amount of work that goes into making a nest varies from one type of bird to another.

Scrape nests

A scrape nest is just what it sounds like—a shallow hole in the ground that is scraped out by the bird. Some birds line their scrapes with sticks or leaves, while others lay their eggs right on the ground. Penguins, vultures, and shorebirds, such as gulls and terns, all have scrape nests. Eggs in a scrape nest are usually well camouflaged by the markings on their shells.

Burrows and tree hollows

Some birds, such as kingfishers and puffins, nest in burrows. Some construct their own burrows, while others use burrows that have been abandoned by rabbits or voles.

Many birds, such as woodpeckers, owls, and parrots, make their nests in tree hollows. The male hornbill actually seals the female inside a hollow to protect her from predators while she is incubating her eggs. He feeds her through a small slit just big enough for her beak. The hole is opened again when the chicks have hatched and are ready to leave the nest.

LEFT *A puffin looks out from the safety of its nest burrow in Wales. The burrow is usually about 40 inches (1 m) deep and is lined with feathers, grass, and leaves.*

WOW!

Cup nests

When you think of a bird's nest, you probably think of a cup nest. This is the most common sort of nest and is made from a variety of materials. Cup nests are usually built above the ground, most often in trees or bushes.

Generally, a bird uses anything it can find to weave its nest. Grass, leaves, and twigs are most common, but birds have also used trash from humans, such as candy wrappers. A bird lines the inside of the nest with soft materials, such as discarded feathers and bits of animal fur. A hummingbird's nest, which is the smallest nest in the world, may be made from spider webs and moss.

LEFT *African weaver birds make complex hanging nests by weaving together blades of grass and other materials.*

ABOVE *Bald eagles, such as this one in Florida, can make huge nests of wood in the branches of trees.*

Bird world

Birds are remarkable creatures. There are around 9,000 different kinds of birds living all over the world. They soar in the mountains, raise their chicks in the polar cold, glide over the ocean waves, hunt in the deserts and forests, and sing in our gardens.

Birds range in size from tall ostriches running across the grasslands of Africa to tiny hummingbirds darting from flower to flower in the Americas. They may live in flocks, or groups. For example, as many as one million quelas (an African finch) may flock. Other birds are more solitary, such as the rare condor.

For millions of years, migrating birds, such as these whooping cranes in North Dakota, have criss-crossed the planet in search of feeding grounds and nesting sites.

Birds of a feather

Wherever they live, whatever their size and their habits, all birds have some things in common. They have two legs, two wings, and a bill. The females lay eggs. And most importantly, they all have feathers. No other living thing in the world has feathers. These combined qualities are what make birds unique.

Birds in the world

Like every other living thing, birds play their part in the natural world. There are birds that hunt, whether they hunt small creatures such as insects or much bigger prey such as snakes and monkeys. Some birds are hunted themselves—many animals rely on birds and their eggs and chicks for food. Without birds, the natural world would be out of balance.

The hyacinth macaw is one of the most spectacular, and one of the most endangered, birds of the Amazon rain forest.

Endangered birds

Birds may be able to fly, but they can't escape from every danger. As human populations grow and demand more space, other living things find themselves being pushed out of their habitats.

Over 400 different types of birds are considered to be endangered, and many may already be extinct. The American ivory-billed woodpecker hasn't been seen since 1997, although some people believe it still survives somewhere. Other birds will need a lot of help from humans in order to survive.

Glossary

Adaptation A feature of a living thing that makes it better suited to its particular lifestyle; the ability to fly is an adaptation of most birds.

Albumen The "white" of an egg surrounding the yolk in the middle; albumen is actually clear and colorless and helps protect the growing chick.

Calcium A mineral that is a necessary part of living things; it is found in bones, teeth, and in the shells of eggs.

Camouflage Colors or patterns on a bird or other animal that make it hard to see against its surroundings.

Cloaca The final part of the bird's digestive system where anything undigested is stored before it is expelled.

Clutch A group of eggs laid in a nest at about the same time.

Contour feathers Smooth, flat feathers that give the bird its shape and color.

Coverts Small feathers that cover the place where the primary feathers attach to the wing.

Crop Part of a bird's digestive system where food can be stored temporarily.

Display What a male bird does to attract the attention of a female or to warn off a male rival.

Down feathers Small, soft, and fluffy feathers that lie close to the bird's skin and keep it warm.

Drag The force that slows down an object as it travels through the air, caused by friction with the air.

Forage To search for food.

Gizzard A strong and muscular part of a bird's digestive system where food is ground down and broken up; the second part of the bird's two-part stomach (see proventriculus).

Gliding Flying a short distance without flapping the wings.

Incubate To sit on eggs to keep them warm and hatch them.

Keratin A strong, flexible material in feathers, hair, horns, and scales.

Lift The upward force that keeps a bird and airplanes in the air.

Molting The process by which a bird's old, damaged feathers are replaced with new ones; a complete molt may take from a few weeks to a few years, depending on the bird.

Pellet Indigestible part of a meal, such as fur and bones, that is spit out by birds, such as owls.

Powder down   A type of fine down feathers that break up to form a fine powder—like talcum—that birds, such as herons and egrets, spread over their feathers to help waterproof and clean them.

Plumage   All the feathers of a bird.

Preen gland   A gland near a bird's tail; it produces oil that the bird uses to waterproof its feathers.

Preening   What a bird does to clean and groom its feathers.

Primary feathers   The outermost feathers of a bird's wing; the primaries are strong and flexible to propel the bird through the air.

Proventriculus   The first part of a bird's two-part stomach, where the process of digestion begins.

Secondary feathers   The wing feathers closest to the bird's body; the secondaries form a curved surface that provides the lift the bird needs to stay in the air.

Soaring   Flying long distances without flapping the wings. Birds that soar use natural air currents, such as warm air rising, to keep them up.

Syrinx   A bird's voice box, similar to the vocal cords, or larynx, of humans; the syrinx vibrates and produces the sounds a bird makes when it sings.

Territory   The area a bird or other animal lives in and defends from others; many birds sing to let other birds know where their territory is.

Trachea   Another name for the windpipe that leads from the mouth to the lungs.

Vane   The flat part of the feather that grows from either side of the central shaft.

Yolk   The yellow part of the egg; it provides food for the chick growing inside.

Web sites

www.pbs.org/lifeofbirds
Web site based on the television series *The Life of Birds,* presented by David Attenborough, full of fascinating facts about birds.

www.birds.cornell.edu/AllAboutBirds
Information on birds and birdwatching in North America.

www.pitt.edu/~dziadosz
View nesting birds through real time Webcams, broadcasting scenes of birds' nests around the world.

www.learnbirdsongs.com
Includes audio files of the songs and calls of many common birds of North America.

http://birdix.com
Information on all the birds of the world.

Index